Creative W...

17

Creative Wool

Making Woollen Crafts with Children

Karin Neuschütz

Photographs by Thomas Wingstedt

Floris Books

Translated by Susan Beard

First published in Swedish as *Ull, Garn Och Barn*
by Forma Publishing Group AB in 2011
Published in English by Floris Books in 2011

© 2011 Karin Neuschütz and Ica Bokförlag, Forma Publishing Group AB
English version © 2011 Floris Books
Photographs by Thomas Wingstedt
Illustrations by Karin Neuschütz

British Library CIP Data available
ISBN 978-086315-800-1
Printed in China

Contents

Foreword

Ever since I was a child I have been captivated by handicrafts and making things. I think it's fascinating to go into a workshop or studio and see how things are created. From early on my bedroom was filled with different materials and strange projects, such as a system of strings criss-crossing the room, or a five metre-long braid made on a Knitting Nancy. At school my friends and I used to parade around in jumpers we had designed and made ourselves.

The satisfaction of making something with your own hands is a very basic feeling, connected to our need for survival. By being able to weave and knit we have given ourselves clothes for warmth, covers to sleep under and mats for the floor.

In this book I want to show what adults and children working together can produce from wool (both spun and unspun) on a small scale: toys, friendship bracelets and braids, balls, dolls and animals. The book starts with descriptions of the basic methods of spinning wool, crocheting and knitting.

My hope is, naturally, that many children and their parents, as well as early years teachers, will be smitten by the joy of working with wool, and that many delightful and original objects will be the result of their handiwork.

Karin Neuschütz

Introduction

A short while ago there was a bundle of unspun wool on the table; now there's a beautiful ball in front of you. 'Have you made it yourself?' someone asks in admiration. You nod modestly and mutter, 'Oh, it's nothing special,' while inside you swell with pride, delighted by their admiration.

Natural materials such as wool, cotton and linen are very rewarding to work with because of their elasticity and high quality. It's especially gratifying to spin fleece into yarn to use for crafts. People have been using wool for at least 7,000 years. In the Pazyryk tombs in the Altai Mountains of Siberia, fantastic felted and woven items have been discovered, dating back 2,500 years.

When you go to buy yarn in the shop, you hardly think about how it's been made, until, with your own simple spindle, you try to spin your own — and develop a greater respect for what a spun thread actually is.

To succeed you must practise. Practising strengthens your initiative and develops your ability to persevere despite a few disappointments at the beginning. And you can be sure the yarn will break over and over again until you've learned the technique! From the yarn you have spun, you can connect stitch to stitch, and a piece of fabric will appear, crocheted or knitted.

There's a certain logic involved in creating a hand-crafted item. The different steps follow one another in an exact order, and thinking you can miss one out is not an option. It's not easy to go back and change a mistake you've made in your knitting — instead you have to undo it and start again. This means you must work with heightened concentration and follow closely as the work grows. A good end result depends on accuracy and perseverance throughout the process, from the very beginning to the finished item. That is why crafts are such a discipline. The visible results can provide inspiration and encouragement, making you feel more creative in other areas too. At school, pupils can be stimulated by their craft achievements and as a result achieve better grades in academic subjects.

Creative work offers countless opportunities for training your ability to imagine what a finished object will look like, to think three-dimensionally: 'What will this look like if I decrease a few stitches here and cast on the same number of stitches in the next row?' 'Will these six pieces really make up a box?' 'What will be the shape of this cat's nose if I increase a few stitches here?'

Another valuable quality of craftwork and needlework is their meditative character. When you have learned to plait or crochet well, you can 'rest' in the familiar process and find that at times your hands are working without you having to think about what they need to do. Then your thoughts can wander freely or be completely still. You are not affected by anxiety or an endless inner dialogue because craftwork demands enough concentration to stop your mind wandering on to problems and worries. You are simply there, in the middle of the plaiting or crochet, your hands comfortably warm from the rhythmic movement.

So, let's get going!

Spinning

Hand-twisted fleece

MATERIALS

Carded, long-fibred fleece

1. Prepare the fleece by gently pulling it out into a long, loose strand. You need two people for this, standing opposite each other, both holding the middle of the wool strand.

2. Both begin to twist the fleece clockwise. As soon as the wool between you looks like coarse yarn, move your hands (and yourselves) further away from each other along the strand. Continue to twist. If the wool is too thick in places pull it out so that it becomes thinner.

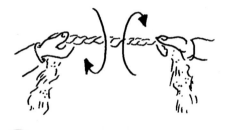

3. Finally you will have twisted the whole piece of fleece. A third person then takes hold of it in the middle while the two who have been doing the twisting walk towards each other, keeping the yarn taught. Bring the ends together. Then release the middle and the yarn will twist back on itself to become two-ply.

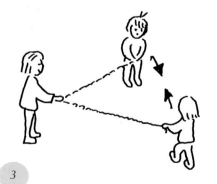

Cleaned, carded and dyed wool ready for use

TIP

One person can hand-twist a short length of fleece. Fix the end of a length of fleece to a door handle, for example, twist 1 m (3 3/4 ft), take hold of the spun yarn in the middle, bring the ends together and then let go of the middle.

Making a spindle

Straight stick, 20–30 cm (8–12 in) long (a chopstick is good) for the stem

Small metal hook

Round weight, 6–7 cm (2 1/2 in) in diameter, 1 cm (1/2 in) thick, for the base or whorl — use beeswax, Cernit modelling clay, or a clay that hardens as it dries

Knife or pencil sharpener

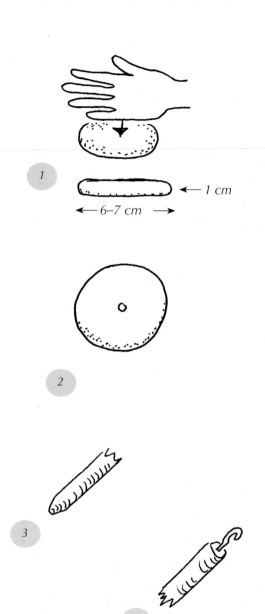

1. Mould the weight into a flattened, circular whorl (knead beeswax first).

2. Sharpen one end of the stem slightly.

3. Use the stem to bore a hole in the exact centre of the whorl. Let it harden (bake Cernit for 10 minutes).

4. Screw the hook into the blunt end of the stem.

5. Attach the whorl to the stem. If it's loose, make the end of the stem thicker by winding some cotton thread or adhesive tape around it.

TIP

The whorl can also be made from a circular piece of wood with a hole drilled in the middle. Or if you have nothing else, use an onion! See the photograph opposite.

Homemade spindles with whorls made from different materials: left, a red onion (NOTE: limited life span!); centre, yellow Cernit clay; right, beeswax.

Using a spindle

MATERIALS

Spindle, large and heavy for thick yarn, small
  and light for fine sewing thread
Unspun sheep's wool, preferable with long
  fibres, washed and carded

1. Pull the wool fibres apart to form a long loose
strand. Take hold of the end of the strand with
your left hand and lay the rest of the wool over
your shoulder. Be careful to keep the unspun
fleece over your arm and shoulder, out of the way,
so that it doesn't get caught in the twisting thread
as you spin.

2. Hold the spindle in your right hand and fasten
the hook in the fleece. With your left hand hold
the fleece just above the hook. Pull the spindle
gently to stretch the wool into a thin string and
start the spindle turning.

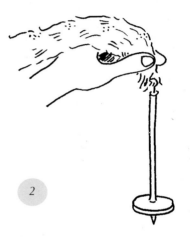

3. The twist will start to travel upwards. Hold the
fleece wide between the fingers and thumb of the
left hand so that a triangular shape forms between
your thumb and the top of the twist (twist point).
Your right hand should alternate quickly between
spinning the spindle and gently drawing down
more fibres from the fleece held in your left hand.
Pinch the thread just below the twist point to pull
out a few more centimetres of wool as your left
hand releases a little more from above.

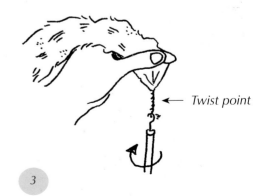

← Twist point

4. When you've spun about 40 cm (16 in) remove the end of the yarn from the hook and tie it to the stem of the spindle just above the whorl. Then wind the yarn around the stem close to the whorl. When you have about 20 cm (8 in) of spun yarn left wrap it in a spiral up towards the top of the stem. When it reaches the top fasten it in the hook.

4

5. Continue spinning in stages so that when the spindle almost reaches the floor you stop and wind the yarn round the stem, and so on. Each time you draw more fleece with your right hand, release the grip of the left hand slightly so that more wool can be pulled out. As soon as the right hand lets go of the yarn to turn the spindle, pinch the wool with the left hand to stop the twist travelling up into the fleece.

5

6. If the thread breaks, join it by drawing down and spreading out some fibres from the fleece. Lay this over the unspun end of the twisted yarn so that there is plenty of overlap. Holding the join, give the spindle a turn so that the ends twist together.

TIP

It's important not to let the twist travel up above the left hand's grip on the fleece because the yarn will suddenly become very thick and difficult to handle. It's equally important to keep the spindle turning all the time, otherwise it will start to turn backwards, the thread will untwist and yarn will break.

6

Spinning a two-ply yarn

MATERIALS

2 balls of home-spun yarn
2 glass jars or deep bowls
Spindle

1. Wind the single-ply yarn you have just spun on the spindle into a ball. Stand the spindle in a stable bowl to help you wind the ball. Then spin enough wool to make another ball

2. Lay each ball in its own glass jar or bowl, and place them behind you on the floor, at least 1 m (3 3/4 ft) apart.
   Pull the ends of each ball up over your shoulders, one thread on each side.
   Bring the ends together, tie into an eyelet and hook this on to the spindle.
   Set the spindle turning in the OPPOSITE direction from when you made the single-ply yarn. Now both threads will twist together to form a two-ply yarn. As soon as the spindle reaches the floor, wind the thread around the stem of the spindle as before.
   Carry on twisting the yarn until one or other of the balls is used up.
   Wind the yarn from the spindle into a ball — and get knitting!

TIP

You can see which way the yarn has been spun: a Z twist, where the thread of the yarn runs from top right to bottom left, like the middle of a Z = the whorl of the spindle has been turned clockwise, to the right. An S twist, with the thread running from top left to bottom right, like a letter S = the spindle has been turned anti-clockwise, to the left.

Crochet and Knitting

Finger crochet

MATERIALS

Small amount of yarn

1. Tie a loop at one end of the yarn.

2. Hold the knot between the thumb and index finger of one hand. Hold the yarn that comes from the ball tightly inside your hand with your ring and little finger.

3. Put the thumb and index finger of your other hand through the loop.

4. Hook the yarn with your index finger and pull it through the loop. Hold on to the end and pull the first loop tight. Repeat!

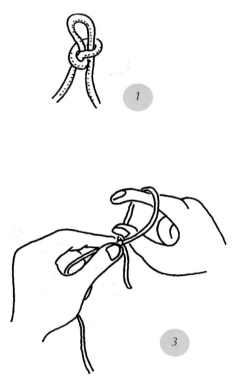

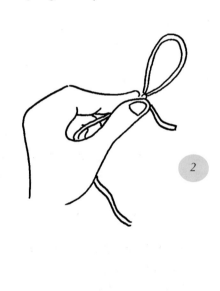

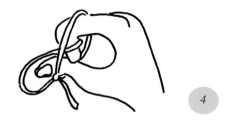

Crocheting

MATERIALS

Small amount of fairly thick yarn
Crochet hook the right size for the yarn, 4–5 mm
   (US 6–8)

1. Make a loop as for finger crochet. Hold the knot between your thumb and index finger and draw the loop just tight enough to fit the crochet hook.

   Push the hook through the loop. Hook up yarn from the ball by bringing the hook under the yarn and then twisting the hook so that its 'nose' is turning downwards. Pull the hook and the yarn back through the loop and draw the loop tighter if it's too big.

2. Foundation chain: Make a new loop with the crochet hook and pull it through the previous stitch. Move your hand up the chain from time to time as it becomes longer.

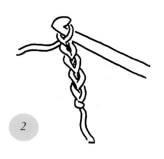

3. Single crochet: Insert the hook through a stitch on the previous row, wrap the yarn over the hook and pull it through the stitch so that you have 2 stitches on the hook. Catch hold of the yarn again and pull it through both stitches.

   Insert the hook into the next stitch and repeat.

4. Slip-stitch: Insert the hook through 2 stitches in the previous row. Wrap the yarn over the hook and draw it through both stitches. Now you have a new stitch on the hook.

5. Double crochet: This gives a more open crochet. Before you insert the hook between both loops of a stitch, wrap the yarn round the hook once. Pull through to give 3 stitches on the hook. Hook the yarn again and pull it through the first 2 stitches. Hook the yarn around again and pull it through the 2 remaining stitches. At the end of the row make 2 chain stitches before turning.

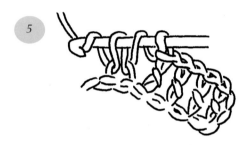

TIP

When you crochet you can decide whether to insert the hook through both loops of the stitch or only one. If you choose to insert the hook in the front loop of the stitch all the time your work will be thinner and looser, but form lines on the other side. To avoid the lines alternate between front and back loops of each stitch as you crochet.

Back stitch loop

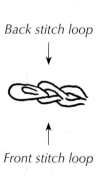

Front stitch loop

Knitting

MATERIALS

Short knitting needles, preferably double-pointed
Yarn
Scissors

1. Casting on: If you already know how to cast on, then you can use the method you are familiar with. The following method corresponds with the diagrams on this page.

Make a loop some way in from the beginning of the yarn. Put the loop on to double needles. Separate the two strands of yarn. Wrap the shorter one round your thumb and the end from the ball around your index finger. Use the other fingers to hold both ends tight.

2. Bring the needles down and insert them in the opening made in front of the thumb. Hook up the yarn from the index finger and take it back through the loop by the thumb. Let go of the loop on the thumb. Insert your thumb again between the strands and separate the thumb and index finger so that the stitches on the needle are pulled tight.

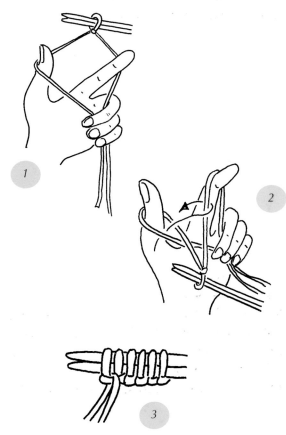

3. Continue making more stitches in this way until you have enough. Gently pull out one of the needles. If you want to increase the number of stitches in the side of a jumper or for a buttonhole, simply wrap the yarn around the needle a few times and knit into them on the way back (see page 62).

4. Plain stitch: Hold the needle with the stitches in your left hand. Insert the right needle from the front into the first stitch on the left needle. Wrap the yarn round the needle and pull it through the stitch.

5. Slide the stitch off the left needle.

6. Purl stitch: Bring the yarn in front of the stitch on the left needle. Insert the right needle into the stitch from behind.

7. Wrap the yarn round the right needle, draw it through the stitch and slide the stitch from the left needle.

8. Casting off: Knit 2 stitches. Pick up the first stitch with the left needle and lift it over the second stitch.

9. The cast-off stitch will now be looped around the second stitch. Continue like this, knitting 1 stitch and casting off the previous one until only 1 stitch is left. Cut the yarn, draw it through the last stitch and pull it tight. Fasten with a darning needle.

TIP

A purl stitch seen from the wrong side = a plain stitch. A plain stitch seen from the wrong side = a purl stitch.

   At the edges of pieces that are going to be sewn together, such a sleeves, the first and last stitch of each row is always a plain stitch, even on purl rows.

   A fun gift for six or seven year-olds: Hide some small presents inside a ball of fairly thick yarn and add a pair of short, sturdy needles.

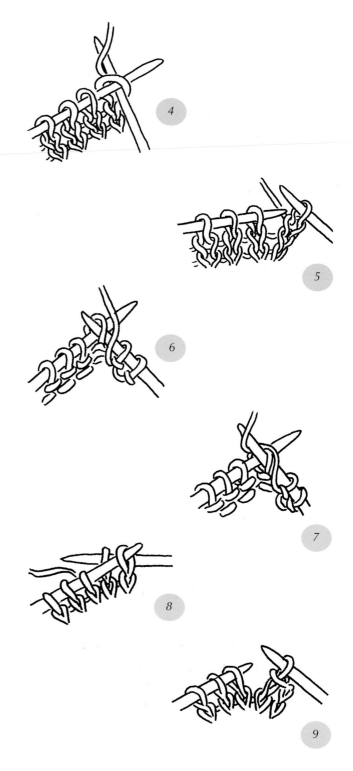

26

Knitting samples. Top left, garter stitch; top right, stocking stitch, showing the wrong side turned up; bottom left, rib stitch; bottom right, moss stitch

Garter stitch: Knit every row in plain stitch. Both sides will look the same.

Stocking stitch: Knit 1 row plain, 1 row purl, alternately. That will give you a right side and a wrong side.

Rib stitch: Knit 1 plain, then 1 purl, to the end of the row. Make sure you knit the same way on each row, so that a plain stitch is above a plain stitch, purl above purl.

Moss stitch: Knit 1 plain, then 1 purl, to the end of the row, but change on the next row so that a purl stitch is above a plain stitch, plain above purl.

Braids

Plaiting

MATERIALS

Thick yarn in 3 colours
Door handle or clamp to hold the work in place

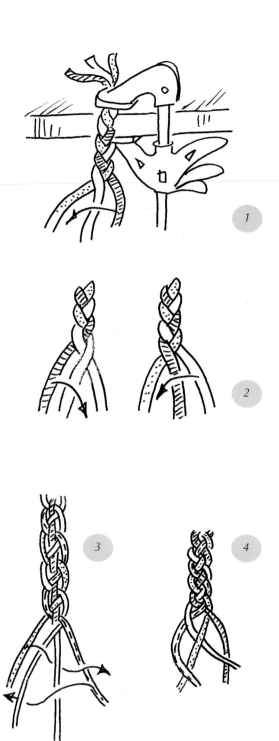

1. Measure 1 m (3 ³/4 ft) of yarn in each colour. Tie all three strands together in a knot at one end. Secure the knot to a door handle or to the edge of the table with the help of a clamp.

2. Plait the three colours together. Always take the outer strand over the middle strand, first the one from the right then the one from the left, alternately. Try to keep all three strands stretched equally tight as you plait.

TIP

Try plaiting with four colours!

3. When you plait with four colours you can either keep one of the strands completely straight in the middle and weave the others alternately over and under it (see third braid from right, page 29)

4. Or plait evenly so that all four strands make the same under and over pattern in the braid (see fourth braid from right, page 29). When you have practised with four strands you can increase to five. That will make a beautiful wide braid.

Figure of eight bracelet

MATERIALS

About 20 strands of cotton yarn, each 1.5 m (5 ft) long, in different colours

A few thick beads (you can make felted ones, see page 53) with holes large enough for the thread

Clamp to hold the work in place

1. For a bracelet, cut about 20 strands, each about 1.5 m (5 ft) long, in different coloured yarn, preferably cotton. All strands should be the same thickness.

Lay all the strands together and tie a thread around the middle to hang them up with.

Hang up the bundle of strands or secure with a clamp on a table in front of you.

2. Choose one of the strands and make a series of half-knots around the bundle of strands on one side. Do the same on the other side. This will form the eyelet to fasten the bracelet on your wrist.

3. When the eyelet is finished choose another strand and start to weave figure of eights between the two bunches of strands. Weave under and over, backwards and forwards, making sure to pull upwards all the time, pushing the loops together. Check often to ensure the reverse of the bracelet is neat and even. Change colour whenever you like, to make stripes.

Figure of eight bracelet. Beads have been threaded on to a single thread running through the middle of the bracelet. One end is finished with two plaits which can be fastened in the eyelet at the other end.

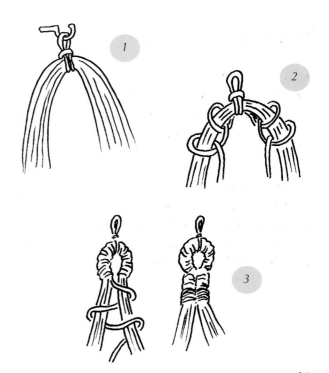

4. After a while you can divide the work into two bundles of strands, which in turn can be divided into two sections where you carry on weaving in a figure of eight. This will make two 'arms' in the pattern.

If you leave one strand in the middle between the two arms you can tie a knot in the strand, thread on a bead, tie another knot and let the strand join the rest when they are all brought together again below the bead.

When you choose a strand to work with, choose the longest one if you have several in the same colour. If an important strand runs out too early you can make a join by simply adding a new strand to the bundle.

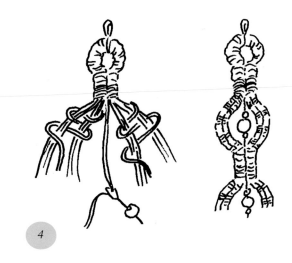

5. Finish by making two pretty plaits of the remaining strands (cut off the ones that are too short to reach to the end of the plait).

These two braids are threaded through the eyelet at the other end to fasten the bracelet.

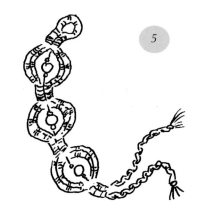

TIP

Use silk thread or embroidery thread for a beautiful result. Beads can be threaded in here and there. If you use really long strands from the beginning you will have enough thread for a necklace.

Four-strand square knotting

MATERIALS

2 long flat leather strips or flat shoelaces, in
    different colours
Keyring (optional)

1. Lay the strips so that they cross each other in
the middle.
    Fold one end, A, diagonally over B, loose
enough to leave room for D.

2. Fold B down over A.

3. Fold C over B.

4. Finally fold D over C, threading it under the
loosely folded section of A.

Continued overleaf

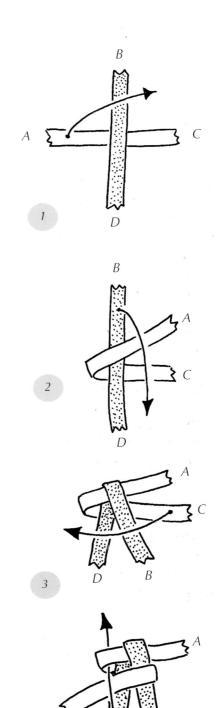

5. Make all four folds even by pulling the ends slightly.

6. On the second layer you fold in the other direction, in other words, each strip is folded back over your work. Start with D, continue with C, B and A.

Carry on folding backwards and forwards for as long as you can or until the braid is long enough.

Cut off the ends that are sticking out. You can glue the final layer if you like, to keep it in place.

TIP

Attach a keyring at the base when you make the first fold.

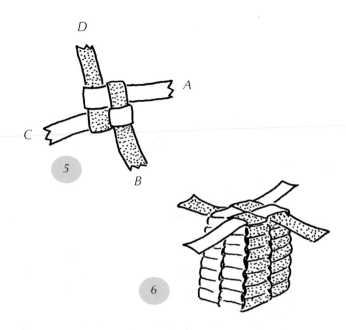

A keyring of four-square knotting, made from one brown and one white shoe lace. Finish by trimming the uneven ends and gluing the last layer.

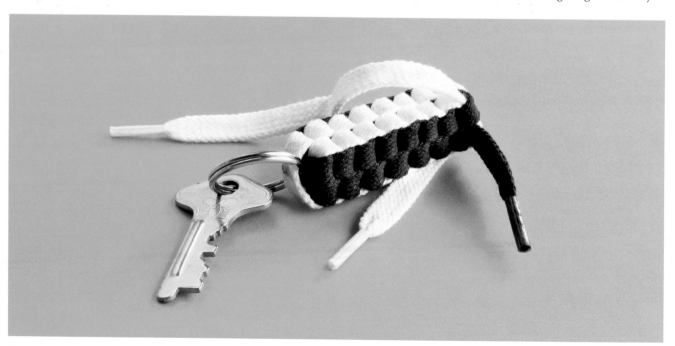

Spiral braid

MATERIALS

Sheet of card or a soft plastic lid, about 10 x 10
   cm (4 x 4 in)
Yarn in 3 different colours, about 4 m (13 ft) of each
Scissors
Thick crochet hook

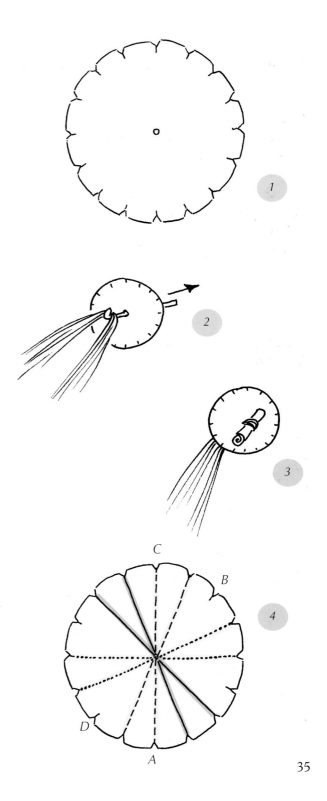

1. Cut a round wheel with a diameter of 8–10 cm
(3–4 in).
   Measure 16 points equally spaced around the circumference. Cut a 0.5 cm (1/4 in) slit at each point
and then cut the top of each side to make a notch.
The slits will hold the yarn in place as you braid.
   Make a hole in the centre of the wheel with
the scissors. Measure two double lengths of each
colour yarn. The length of these doubled strands
of yarn must be twice as long as the finished
work, plus 30 cm (12 in).

2. Push a crochet hook through the hole, hook
the six strands where they are folded and pull
them back through the hole.

3. Push a small piece of rolled-up paper through
the folds to act as a stop.

4. Divide the strands around the edge of the
wheel, one in each notch. Arrange the colours
so that they are in pairs opposite each other,
according to Figure 4. There will be four empty
notches remaining. The long ends will hang down
from the wheel like the tentacles of a jellyfish.
   Now start moving the strands as follows: move
A to B and C to D.

35

5. Move E to F and G to H. Continue moving the strands in this way. Always take the second strand from the bottom in a group of four and move it up into an empty notch next to the same colour, then move down the one in the same colour which is furthest to the left at the top, so that strands of the same colour are once again in pairs diagonally opposite each other.

Stretch the strands so that they sit taught in their notches. When a short braid has been formed in the centre pull the roll of paper on the reverse side so that you can see the braid. It will be a round braid with colours in a spiral pattern.

You can always see in the middle which strand was moved last — it will be uppermost.

When the braid is long enough, disconnect it from the wheel and remove the roll of paper.

TIP

You can make a knot and an eyelet to fasten the necklace (see fifth braid from left, page 28).

6. Knot: Tie all the hanging ends together in a loose knot. Make the knot right where the braid ends.

Thread a needle through one of the strands and sew through the knot twice. Cut off the end and repeat with all the strands. Spread the stitches neatly around the knot.

7. Eyelet: Thread a needle with a new piece of yarn, insert the needle into the braid below the eyelet and wind the thread tightly around the braid up towards the eyelet. Fasten the thread and then sew in buttonhole stitch around the strands of the eyelet. Fasten the thread by sewing back into the braid, then cut it off.

5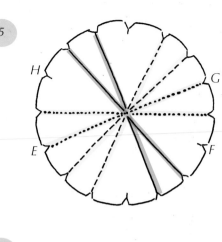

6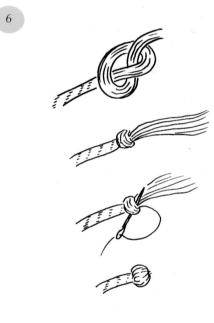

7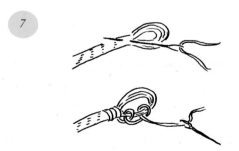

Five-loop finger braiding

MATERIALS

1 m (3 3/4 ft) of yarn in 5 different colours (same
    kind of yarn)
Door handle or clamp to hold the work

1. Prepare 5 double strands of yarn. Tie the 10
ends together so that all the loops are exactly
the same length (about 50 cm, 20 in). Fasten the
knot to a table with the clamp or attach to a door
handle.

   Hold your hands with the palms facing upwards.
Divide the loops between the fingers as follows:
hook 2 on the left hand, on the index and middle
fingers, and 3 on right hand, on the index, middle
and ring fingers. Hold the yarn taught.

2. Insert the left ring finger into the middle finger's
loop (a). Move the middle finger to the index
finger's loop so it contains 2 fingers (b).

3. Turn the left hand over with the back facing
upwards. Bring your hands together, the right
hand still with the palm facing up. Now with the
left index finger hook up the loop on the right ring
finger and bring it through its own loop (use your
thumb to help), at the same time taking the index
finger out of the middle finger's loop.

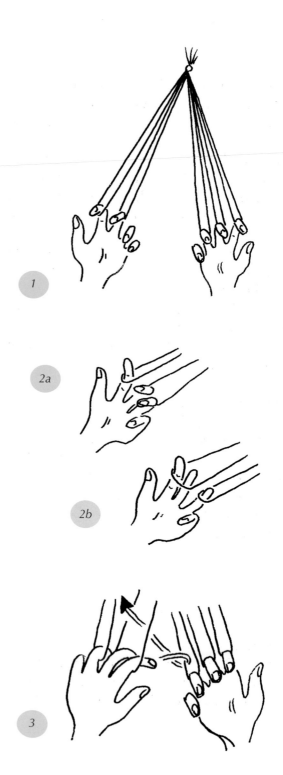

4. Turn your left hand palm upwards again.

Now there is a new loop on the left index finger, so that hand has 3 loops and the right hand only 2.

Now make the same manoeuvre with the right hand: insert the ring finger into the middle finger's loop and then move the middle finger to the loop on the index finger, so that there are 2 fingers in that loop.

Turn your hand over and move it towards the left hand. The right index finger now hooks up the loop on the ring finger of the left hand, pulls it through the shared loop where the middle finger is and now has its own loop. The index finger now has a new loop, the middle finger has one and so does the ring finger.

5. Carry on like this, moving loops between your fingers and bringing the hands together in regular movements. Between each movement separate your hands wide and draw the yarn tight so that the braid will be closely woven. The end result is a plaited braid which looks knitted on one side and is very quick to make. Tie all the strands together at the end.

TIP

Try all sorts of colour combinations! And try making braids with four, six or seven loops using the same technique.

On page 28 you can see two five-loop braids (second and third from left). One shows the side that looks knitted, the other the side that looks plaited.

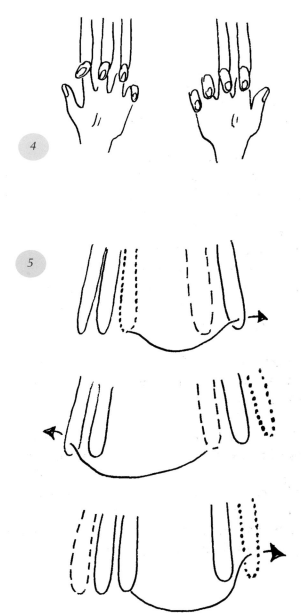

4

5

French knitting

MATERIALS

Old-fashioned wooden cotton reel or an oblong
    piece of wood with a hole from top to bottom
4 small nails with rounded heads
Yarn
Crochet hook

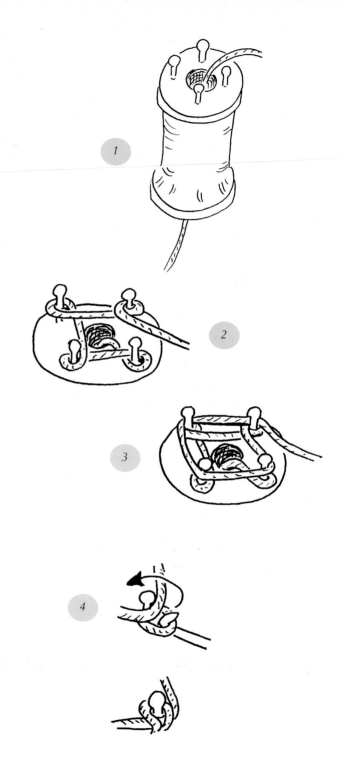

1. Make a knitting spool from a wooden cotton
reel, or drill a hole through an oblong piece
of wood. Knock four nails with rounded heads
into the top around the hole, as shown in the
illustration.
   Using a crochet hook draw the end of the yarn
through the hole so that it hangs down under the
spool.

2. Loop the yarn once around each nail.

3. Wind the yarn in one loop around all four nails
so that it is above the first loops and immediately
below the heads of the nails. Keep the yarn pulled
tight.

4. With the crochet hook lift one individual loop
at a time over the head of the nail so that it comes
above the upper yarn loop.
   When all four loops have been lifted over the
yarn and the nail heads, wrap a new loop around
and again lift the small loops over the yarn with
the help of the crochet hook. Pull the yarn end
down from time to time, and after a while a
beautifully knitted braid will appear from the
base of the knitting spool.

Knitting spools. Left, made from an old-fashioned wooden cotton reel; centre, carved from a piece of wood; right, two brightly-painted old types of knitting spools, also known as Knitting Nancys

TIP

Use a multi-coloured yarn to make a striped braid.

Balls

Pompom

MATERIALS

Piece of card
Woollen yarn in different colours
Thick, blunt needle with a large eye
Strong thread
Nail scissors

1. Cut two circles the same size from the card, the size of your finished pompom. Draw a hole in the centre, roughly a third of the diameter of the card. Cut out the hole using the nail scissors.

2. Lay the card circles one on top of the other. Wind the wool through the hole and around the card, pulling it tight from time to time. Change colour as you like. Continue winding the wool around until you can no longer get your finger through the hole.

3. Thread the wool on to a needle and carry on winding round and round until there is no room for the needle to go through the hole.

4. Cut the wool around the outer edge, working the scissors between the card circles as you cut.

5. Wind a piece of strong thread between the card circles, pull it tight and knot several times. Draw away the card circles. Trim the ball with the scissors to make it completely round.

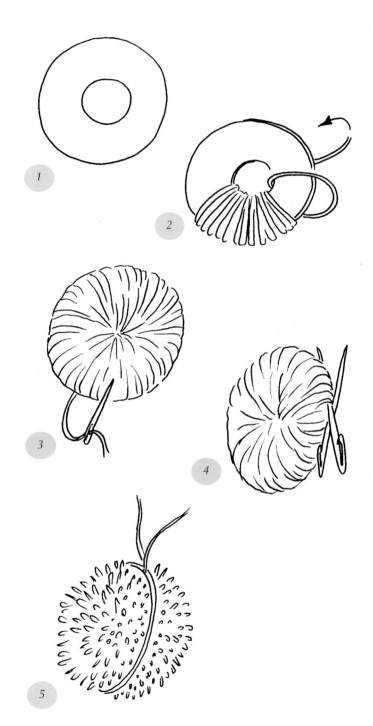

You can sew two pompoms together to make a sweet little rabbit or chick. Behind them is a necklace made of pompoms all the same size. At the front you can see the card circles used and a pompom that has been started using home-spun wool.

Rabbit or chick

1. Make one ball for the body and another, half the size, for the head.

2. Tie the balls together using the strong threads that you used to tie round the middle of the pompoms. Pull the threads tight so that the head does not wobble.

3. Cut two small ears or a beak from felt in a suitable colour (or make felted ones). Fold the base of the ear double and sew along the bottom before stitching it to the head.
   Use a felting needle to make two beads for eyes (see page 53).

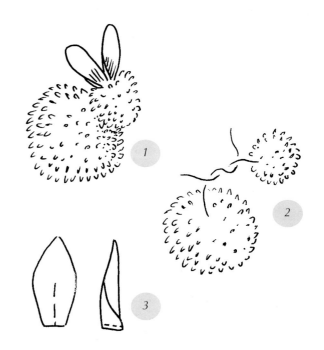

Necklace or bundle of balls

1. You can make several identical small balls without using card circles. Wind about 50 layers of wool, preferably in different colours, around an oblong piece of card.

2. Slide the wool off the card. Using strong thread, tie as tightly as you can at equal distances of about 5 cm (2 in) along the wool. Leave long ends of thread at every knot. Cut the wool between each knot and then neaten the balls with the scissors to make them completely round.

3. Thread the balls on to a string to make a necklace, or hang them in a pretty bunch on your hat.

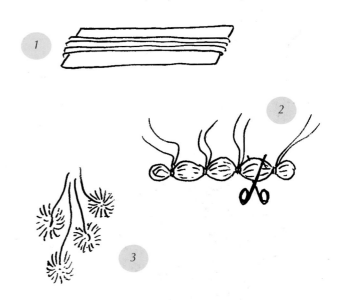

47

Felted ball

MATERIALS

For 3 juggling balls you will need:
4 x 1-litre (1-quart) plastic bags
300 g (10 $\frac{1}{2}$ oz) dry sand, cat litter or rice
   grains
Small ball of yarn
About 100 g (3 $\frac{1}{2}$ oz) unspun wool, preferably
   in different colours
Damp cloth
Soapy water

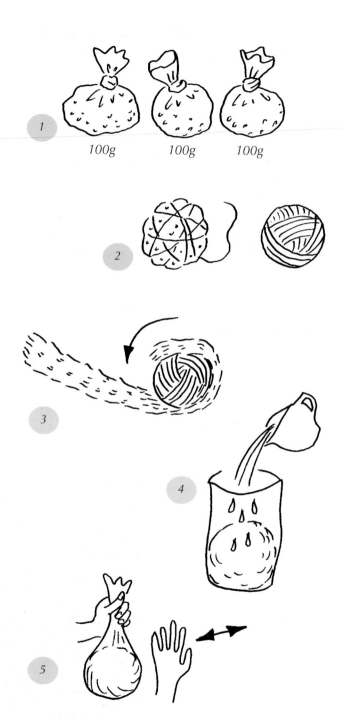

1. Weigh up equal amounts of sand or rice (100 g, 3 $\frac{1}{2}$ oz) in three plastic bags, which you then tie.

2. Wrap yarn around each bag in different directions. Press in any bulges in the bag so that it stays circular, then keep winding the yarn to make a ball.

3. Wrap the ball in the unspun wool which you have pulled out into long thin 10 cm (4 in) wide strips. The ball must be completely covered, pulling the wool tightly in all directions.

4. Place the ball in a plastic bag, pour in a little hot soapy water and knead and turn the ball until it is wet through. Then pour away any excess water.

5. Pat the ball in the bag lightly on all sides for about 3 or 4 minutes. Squeeze and turn the ball all the time, moving it from hand to hand as you do so.

6. Take the ball out of the bag and bounce it up and down in your palm (hold your hand over the sink). Continue patting and squeezing the ball, warming it with hot water from time to time.

When the wool covering looks felted but still seems too big for the ball, roll the ball against a damp cloth on the draining board. Squeeze and turn it in every direction. Continue rolling more and more firmly for at least 10 minutes.

When the ball is solid and round and all the wrinkles have disappeared, rinse the ball carefully under running water and squeeze it out in a towel. Put it somewhere to dry. Get going on the next ball!

Tip

Felt a tennis ball and you get a ball with real bounce! Follow the instructions above from Step 3.

Or have only unspun wool inside the ball, then wind yarn around it and felt it in place. Or take a complete ball of wool and felt it.

Balls at various stages. Left, a plastic bag filled with rice grains; second from left, an inner ball wrapped round with yarn; centre back, a ball of yarn covered in unspun blue wool; centre front, a finished felted ball; right, a ball of wool being embroidered.

Knitted ball

MATERIALS

Remnants of woollen yarn in 3 different colours
Knitting needles, around size 3 mm (US 2–3),
    preferably double-pointed
Handful of unspun sheep's wool
Darning needle

1. Cast on enough stitches to measure 4–5 cm (1 1/2–2 in) on the needle. Knit a square (A) in plain stitch (learn how to knit on page 25).

2. Change colour and continue with square B. Then knit one more square in the first colour (A) and another in the same colour as B. Cast off. Now you have a strip with four squares in two colours.
   On one side of square B (the middle one), using a third colour, pick up the same number of stitches you used before and knit a new square (C) at right angles to the previous ones. Cast off. Pick up stitches along the opposite side of square B and knit the last and sixth square, in the same colour as C. Cast off.

3. Secure all the loose ends using the needle. Fold in and sew the sides together with the yarn so that you have a box with an open lid.

4. Roll unspun wool into a ball and wind yarn around it so that it looks like a ball of wool. Or take an existing ball of wool of the right size. The ball should look a little too big for the knitted case, which will stretch.

5. Put the ball of wool into the knitted case and sew up the opening.

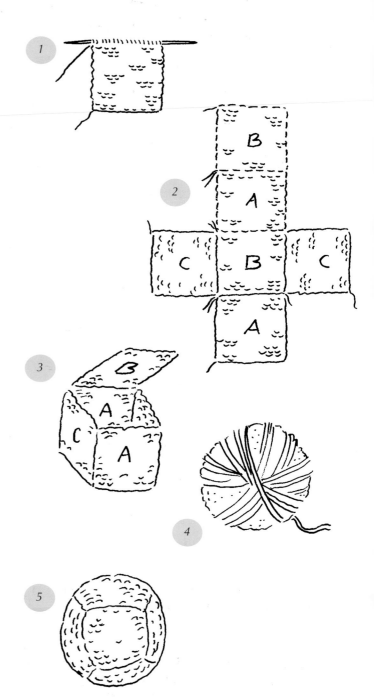

50

You can wrap the wool in strips of fabric instead of yarn to make the ball heavier.

Small children usually like really large balls, in which case you can have 100–200 g (3 1/2–7 oz) of wool inside the ball, which you wrap in yarn or fabric strips, and knit larger squares for the case.

Embroidered ball

MATERIALS

Ball of yarn
Embroidery thread, preferably wool, in various
    colours
Embroidery needle
Scissors

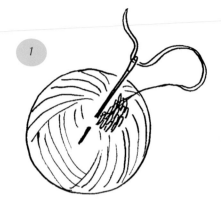

1. Wind some old yarn that you don't need for
knitting into a ball. If you want to save the yarn
you can use unspun wool as a filling instead,
which you wrap round with yarn.
    Thread a darning or embroidery needle with
some pretty embroidery thread and sew stripes or
patches in various embroidery stitches.

2. Chain stitch gives a neat finish and covers well.

3. Stem stitch is easy to sew.
    Cover the whole ball in embroidery.

TIP

Woollen yarn deflects dirt better than cotton.
Tightly-spun yarn is the most hard wearing.
    You can see a ball embroidered in yellow and
red on page 42.

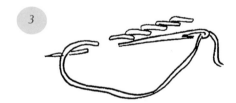

Felted beads

Small tufts of unspun sheep's wool in different
  colours
Foam (such as a bath sponge)
Fine-gauge felting needle
Needle and strong thread
Necklace clasp

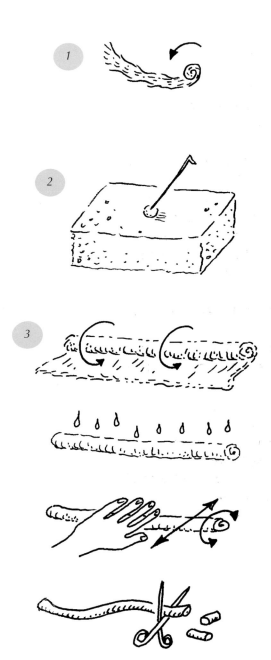

1. Roll some very fine unspun wool into a tiny ball.

2. Lay the ball on the foam base. Carefully stab the felting needle right through the little ball, turning it often and stabbing from all angles. Mind your fingers!

When the ball starts to look more or less round, massage it between your fingers, very gently at first and then harder between the palms of your hands.

Any unevenness can be worked on with the felting needle — insert it several times where the wool is too lumpy. When the bead is hard and round it can be threaded on to strong thread to make a necklace.

TIP

Alternate beads of felt and glass give a very pretty effect.

3. You can also make oblong beads by rolling a long, wide strip of wool lengthwise. Dampen the roll with soapy water and roll it against a wet dishcloth, loosely at first, then with increased pressure for a few minutes, until it forms a round sausage shape. Rinse and cut into shorter pieces.

Dolls

Woollen doll

MATERIALS

Piece of card, approximately 6 x 8 cm (2 ½ x 3 ½ in)

Thin woollen yarn in bright colours for clothes and hair

Embroidery silk or sewing thread in a contrasting colour (optional)

Darning needle

Scissors

Double-pointed knitting needle

For Christmas elf: unspun wool for hair and beard, red felt for the hat, red sewing thread

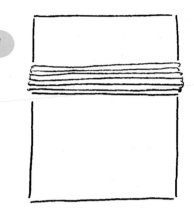

1. Wind the wool 10 times around the width of the card to make the arms. Cut the end and slide the wool off the card.

2. Thread the darning needle with the embroidery silk. Insert the knitting needle through one end of the wound wool and spread it out so that it is evenly distributed along the needle. Wind the embroidery silk tightly around the doll's wrist and sew a couple of stitches through the wrist to hold it in place. Cut off the end of the embroidery silk.

3. Now wind wool around the length of the card to make the head, body and legs. Wind two sections, with more layers than for the arms — 15 layers, for example — for each leg. Tie a bow around each foot and around the head to keep the wool together. Slide it off the card.

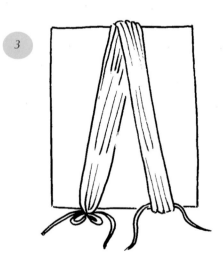

4. Wind a small ball of the same wool for the head. Keep a long end, thread it through the darning needle and sew a few stitches through the head. Keep the needle threaded. Place the head inside the head/legs loops, at the top. Insert the arms directly below the head.

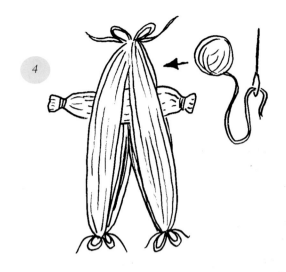

5. Wind the threaded wool around the waist and sew through the waist a couple of times. Push the needle up through the arms and the head and back down to the neck. Wind the wool around the neck two or three times and fasten through the neck. Sew through the head a few extra times if you like, to keep it stable.

Make feet the same way as for the hands, or cut through the leg loops to make a skirt. Wrap and sew decorative edges around the waist and neck using embroidery silk.

TIP

Turn your doll into a Christmas elf by choosing red or green wool for the doll and sewing on a beard and hair made of unspun wool. Make the hat from a triangular piece of felt (Figure 6). Sew it on to the head securely otherwise it will fall off and get lost. Measure around the head to make sure the hat is the correct size.

You can see different kinds of woolen dolls on page 54.

circumference of the head

Knitted doll

MATERIALS

Small ball of flesh-coloured yarn
Yarn for leggings/underpants
Yarn for hair
Thread for mouth and eyes
Unspun wool for stuffing the doll
Double-pointed needles, 2–3 mm (US 0–2)
Thin stick

1. Head, body and legs: Start at the top with flesh-coloured yarn. Cast on 16 stitches or the right number to fit the template on page 60. Knit in stocking stitch (see page 27). Knit until you have a piece slightly longer than it is wide (about 26 rows).

Change to the yarn for the leggings/underpants. Tie the ends of the yarn together at one side and carry on in stocking stitch (about 8 rows). Divide the work to knit one leg at a time. You will be knitting half the number of stitches (about 8) backwards and forwards (the other half will stay on the needle). Knit a length of your choice for the leg of the underpants, then change back to flesh-coloured yarn and knit the leg all the way down to the bottom. The leg must be as long as the body and the head. Cast off at the foot.

Knit the other leg exactly the same.

Arms: Cast on about 6 stitches in flesh-coloured yarn, or fewer stitches than for the leg, and knit in stocking stitch until the arm is roughly as long as the body. Cast off.

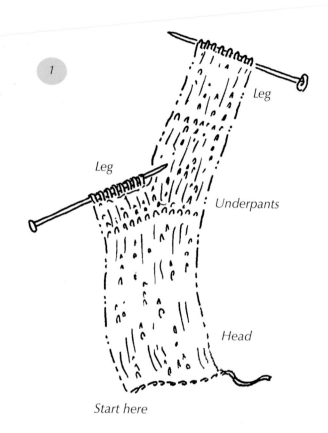

Start here

The large doll is made twice the size of the template, knitted with double the number of stitches and rows. You can see the seam on the back of the doll lying down on the right.

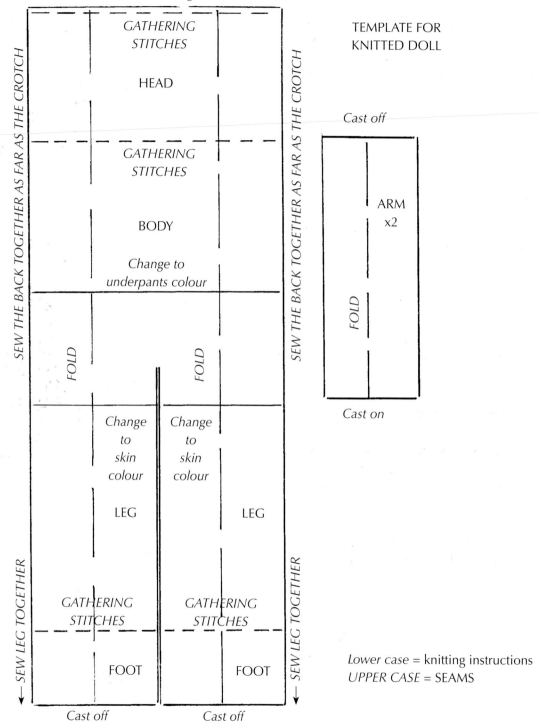

Begin at the top.
Cast on in stocking stitch.

TEMPLATE FOR
KNITTED DOLL

GATHERING STITCHES

HEAD

GATHERING STITCHES

BODY

Change to underpants colour

SEW THE BACK TOGETHER AS FAR AS THE CROTCH

SEW THE BACK TOGETHER AS FAR AS THE CROTCH

Cast off

ARM
x2

FOLD

Cast on

FOLD

FOLD

Change to skin colour

LEG

Change to skin colour

LEG

SEW LEG TOGETHER

SEW LEG TOGETHER

GATHERING STITCHES

GATHERING STITCHES

FOOT

FOOT

Cast off

Cast off

Lower case = knitting instructions
UPPER CASE = SEAMS

60

2. When all the pieces have been knitted, fold in the sides of the body and sew the back seam down to where the legs begin. The legs are sewn individually. Leave openings at the top of the body and at the feet.

Stuff the body and legs with unspun wool, using a thin stick to help.

Run a row of gathering stitches around the top of the head and pull tight to close. Sew each foot together.

Run a row of gathering stitches around the neck and pull tight (just above halfway between the top of the head and the waist of the leggings/underpants). Secure the neck thread.

3. Sew the arms together from the right side (they are difficult to turn) and stuff with unspun wool using the stick. Attach the arms just below the neck. Wind and secure a thread around each wrist.

4. Sew the eyes and mouth with sewing thread or fine yarn, or attach some unspun wool with a felting needle. Lay the hair yarn across the head from side to side and fasten it with a parting and side seams, or attach a fringe first before you lay the hair across.

5. You can also sew on a mop of hair using a tuft of unspun wool or tangled yarn.

TIP

Try sewing a doll using cotton-knit fabric instead, cutting it according to the template on page 60.

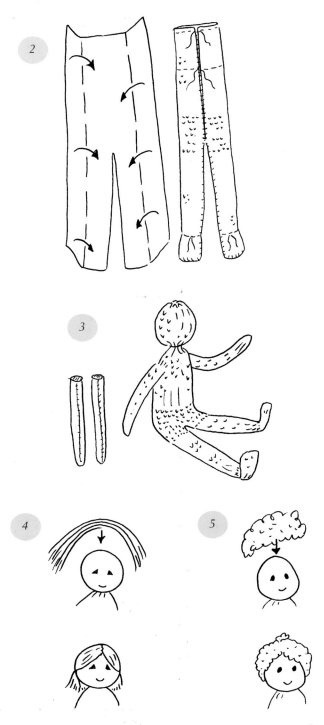

Knitted pants (trousers) and jumper

MATERIALS

Yarn, ideally thin wool
2 double-pointed knitting needles, size 2–3 mm
(US 0–2)
Scissors and darning needle

PANTS (TROUSERS)

1. Measure the length of the pants (trousers) on the doll from waist to feet. Cast on about 20 stitches and knit a sample of 3 rows to make sure the size is correct. If not, start again using more or fewer stitches on the needle (see knitting instructions on page 25).

Knit about 20 rows plain, or until the trouser leg is big enough to go round the leg of the doll. Cast off one leg up to the crotch.

2. On the next row cast on the same number of stitches as you cast off by making half-stitches on the needle with the wool, as in the diagram. Knit the same number of rows for the second leg as for the first. Cast off along the length of the pants.

3. Fold in and sew each leg, then sew from the crotch to the waist. Fasten and cut off the loose ends.

JUMPER

1. Begin at the bottom of the front section. Cast on about 12 stitches, knit plain for a few rows and see if it's the right size. If not, start again.

Knit up to the arms (about 16 rows). Cast on about 8 new stitches for one arm (see step 2 of the

TROUSERS

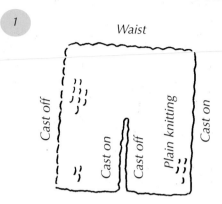

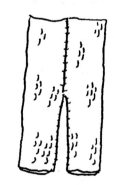

Left, crocheted shawl (crochet 2 rows in double crochet, add an edging all round by making 3 foundation chain stitches, crocheting into 1 stitch, making another 3 chain stitches, crocheting into the next stitch, and so on); top centre, crocheted hats; top and bottom right, crocheted dresses (see page 64); centre, knitted jumper and pair of pants (trousers); bottom left, woven bag.

previous pattern), knit back to the other side and cast on 8 stitches for the other arm.

Knit the arms and the front in one piece up to the neck (about 8 rows). Cast off for the neck on one row and cast on the same number of stitches on the next row.

Knit the back exactly the same as the front. Cast off 8 stitches for each arm at the sides. Knit the lower half of the back. Cast off and secure the wool.

Fold the jumper over and sew the side seams.

TIP

The clothes will be slightly thinner and more pliable if knitted in stocking stitch. If you decide to do this, knit a small edge in garter stitch at the bottom.

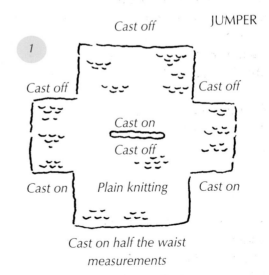

Cast on half the waist measurements

Crocheted dress

MATERIALS

Thin knitting wool
Crochet hook, 3 mm (US C/2 or D/3)

1. Crochet a foundation chain to make a braid long enough to go round the waist of the doll (using a crochet hook, see page 23). Join the braid with a stitch to make a circle.

Crochet round and round for a few rows in single crochet. This will be the bodice of the dress.

Work the skirt in double crochet: on the first 2 rows increase by working 2 double crochet stitches in every other stitch.

On the third row work double crochet in each stitch. Continue in this way to the bottom of the skirt.

Finish with 2 rows of single crochet and then a couple of rows of chain stitch (see page 23).

TIP

Make crochet straps for the skirt in foundation chain. You could try crocheting pants (trousers) and a jumper following the shape of the templates on pages 62–63.

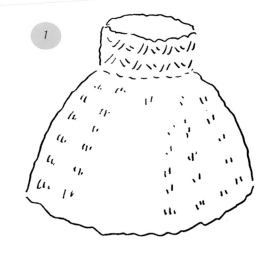

The girl's eyes and mouth have been added with a felting needle and the boy's eyes are made from sewn-on dots. The girl's pink leggings have been knitted in one piece with the body. Instructions for the woven bag are on page 67.

Crocheted hat

MATERIALS

Thin woollen yarn
Crochet hook, 3 mm (US C/2 or D/3)

1. Crochet enough chain stitches to fit the doll's head. Work 2 rows in single chain. Shape the hat by missing out every third stitch for one row and then every other stitch until you have formed the hat shape. Fasten the wool. Put a small pompom on top of the hat.

2. To make a hat brim: Crochet several rows round the base of the hat, increasing by crocheting twice in the same stitch every third stitch.

Woven bag

MATERIALS

Rectangular piece of card, the size of the
    finished bag
Scissors
Thick blunt needle with large eye
Yarn in several colours, the right thickness for
    the needle

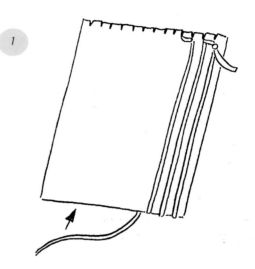

1. Cut small notches along one short edge of the
card about 1/2 cm (1/4 in) apart.
    Wind the yarn once around the card lengthwise,
tie it and place the knot at the top by the first
notch. Run the yarn through the second notch,
down the back, round the lower edge and up over
the front to the second notch. From this notch run
the yarn behind to notch number three and then
down the front, around the bottom and up the
back to notch number three.

2. Continue until the whole piece of card is
covered with vertical warp threads on both sides.
    Finish with a single thread which runs down
to the bottom, and tie it to the previous strand.
This will give a different number of warp threads
on each side, meaning you can weave round the
piece of card, using both sides.

Continued overleaf

3. Thread the darning needle with the weaving yarn and start weaving from the bottom. Continue weaving with the needle by alternately taking it under and over the vertical warp threads. When you reach the edge, turn the piece of card over and continue weaving on the other side so that the yarn goes around the card all the time. Change colour every so often, to make stripes. When you change yarn, place the new yarn alongside the old for a short distance, making the yarn double.

Tighten the weaving occasionally by pressing down the woven yarn with the help of the needle, or with a wide-toothed comb.

Weave as high up as you can, right up to the loops of the warp threads, and secure the end to the inside of the bag.

Detach the weaving from the card, and you have woven a bag!

Finish the bag by sewing on a shoulder strap made by crocheting in the same yarn, or with a finger braid (see page 38).

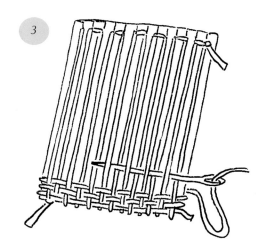

TIP

4. If you do not want to make a bag but a flat piece of work instead, such as a mat, wind the warp around the card but weave backwards and forwards on one side only. When the whole of that side is woven cut the warp threads in the middle of the reverse side, so you have threads of the same length at the top and at the bottom. Knot the ends two and two to make a neat fringe. If there is enough thread you can make several rows of knots.

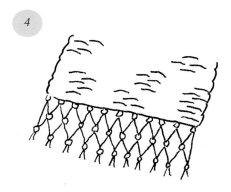

Opposite: Here is Daisy from the book Sewing Dolls (also published by Floris Books), proudly showing us her new bag and mat, woven on pieces of card. You can see the vertical warp threads and some weaving that has just been started.

Animals

Crocheted cat glove puppet

MATERIALS

Yarn in a cat colour
Crochet hook
Small amount of yarn for eyes, nose and whiskers
Fine elastic for the neck
Darning needle

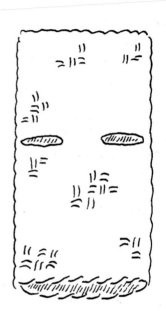

1. Body and head: Crochet a foundation chain long enough to fit easily around your (or the child's) hand. Join into a ring (see page 23 for how to crochet).

Work in single chain, row after row, until the work reaches from the wrist up to the base of the fingers.

Make two holes for the paws at the front: Crochet about 8 foundation chain stitches then miss out an equal number of stitches, attach the chain and crochet 10 single chain stitches between the paws and then another 8 chain stitches that are then attached 8 stitches on in the work.

Continue to crochet round and round until the work reaches above the top of your fingers. Finish by cutting off the yarn, leaving a loose end about 30 cm (12 in) long which you pull through the last stitch.

Paws: Crochet round the opening for the paw, row after row in single chain until the paw is about half as long as your finger. Finish by drawing the yarn through all the stitches and pulling tight. Fasten the yarn. Repeat with the other paw.

2. Face: Crochet in a circle round and round to make a small bowl shape. First crochet twice in the same stitch for 2 rows, then once in each stitch for 1 row and finally miss out every other stitch as you crochet, so that the edge turns up. Attach the little nose to the front, above the paws. Embroider eyes just above the nose section, then the nose and finally the mouth and whiskers. Join the head seam along the top and sew two seams at an angle to mark the base of the ears. Thread fine elastic round the neck.

Tail: Crochet a couple of rows backwards and forwards to make a thick braid and attach it to the back at the base.

3. Hold your fingers like this inside the cat.

TIP

You can make many different kinds of animals in this way. Vary by crocheting a longer nose. See the crocheted animals on page 70.

Crocheted mouse finger puppet

MATERIALS

Grey or brown yarn
Crochet hook
2 small black beads or embroidery thread
Darning needle and scissors

1. Body and head: Crochet the mouse as a tube that fits on your finger. Make a foundation chain the right size to go round the finger, then crochet round and round until it is the length you want. Finally increase for the head by crocheting twice in the same stitch on every third stitch for 3 or 4 rows, until you have a bowl shape at the top.

2. Cut off the yarn leaving a 20 cm (8 in) loose end which you pull through the last stitch. Use the darning needle to sew the wide opening together to form three corners for the nose and ears.

3. Sew on two black beads for the eyes, or embroider them.

4. Paws: Attach the yarn at the side, a little way down from the neck. Make a few foundation chain stitches and crochet back along the arm by taking the yarn around the loop of every chain stitch to make the arm thicker. Secure the end.
Tail: Crochet a narrow braid of chain stitches for a tail and attach it at the back.

TIP

If one of you has the mouse and the other the cat, you can have lots of play conversations with a child.
   Using different colours you can crochet crocodiles and other animals!

74

Felted animals

Unspun wool in suitable colours
Felting needle
Foam base, such as a bath sponge

1. Body: Draw out a strand of wool and fold it as shown.

2. Wrap thin strips of wool around the body and pull fairly tight. Wrap more strips of wool around the length.

3. Stab the felting needle into the woollen body from all angles so that it becomes solid. The body should be quite small at this stage as it will become thicker when you add head and legs.

4. Head: Roll up a small piece of wool, fixing in place occasionally with the felting needle.

5. Lay a loose film of wool over the head with its ends hanging down on each side. Use the needle to fasten it to the head. Wind wool around the hanging ends to form a neck.

6. Spread out the ends and felt them securely to the body with the needle. Lay wool across the ends against the body and fix in place using the needle.
   If you want to make a sitting animal, go on to the instructions for tail and ears and miss out the legs.

7. Legs: Fold a strip double and wrap it tightly in thin woollen strips. Stab all over with the felting needle. Add a little more wool near the top. Roll the leg between your palms.

8. Form a foot or paw at the bottom by stabbing extra hard where the foot curves and from underneath.

9. Tail: Do the same as for the leg but start with a much thinner piece of wool.

10. Attach the legs and the tail by spreading the wool at the ends onto the body, felting them to the body with the needle and then covering over with a piece of wool which is then also felted to the body.

11. Ears: Fold a small film of wool double. Using the needle felt the ear into shape. Turn it over and felt from the other side. Rub the ear between your fingers. Spread out the ends and felt the ear to the head, adding a little more wool to attach it well.

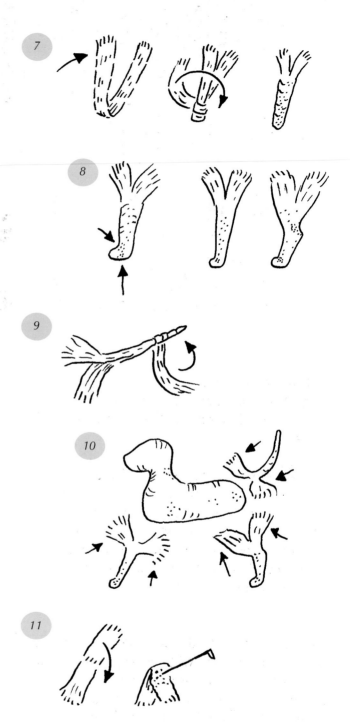

12. Coat: Your animal could have patches or be spotty. Lay thin films of wool in your chosen colour and felt them to the surface with the needle.

13. Eyes and nose: Lay small tufts, a few fibres only, where the eyes and nose are to be and stab with the needle repeatedly around the contours of the eye or nose. The whole eye or nose will then slowly become covered in the colour. Catch the last few fibres in the needle and attach them well. Cut off any excess fibres.

TIP

Sitting animals: Make the body more pear-shaped from the beginning, with a large rear section which is flattened underneath. Do not make any back legs. Give the body a more upright tilt when you attach the head, front legs and tail.

Felted masks

MATERIALS

Coloured unspun wool
Felting needle
Piece of felt approximately 22 x 26 cm (8 $\frac{1}{2}$ x
   10 $\frac{1}{2}$ in)
Scissors
Sponge for a base
Soapy water (1 tsp liquid soap to 1 $\frac{1}{2}$ litres/
   quarts warm water)
Damp cloth

1. Fold the piece of felt double and draw the outline of half an animal face with pencil on the felt. You can make a paper template and draw round that using the patterns on page 80. Cut out the face. Measure the distance between your (or the child's) eyes, mark the eyes on the mask and cut them out.

2. Rest the mask on the sponge base. First cover the entire mask with a fluffy film of wool in the colour of your choice. Felt the fibres with the needle, roughly at first to make it easier to move the fibres if you are unhappy with the result, in which case pull them out and felt them again. When the whole surface has been thoroughly covered make the outlines of the eyes, nose, mouth, eyebrows, etc. Insert the needle carefully and repeatedly, stabbing close together. If you have a felt-making tool with several needles the work will go faster. Go over the whole mask once again so that the wool is attached well.

   Trim the ragged wool around the edge then wet the mask in warm soapy water. Squeeze it